Alphabet Zen

poems

Bing He

We acknowledge the support of the Canada Council for our publishing program.
We also acknowledge support from the Ontario Arts Council.

ONTARIO ARTS COUNCIL
CONSEIL DES ARTS DE L'ONTARIO

Cover art, *Muse,* by Bing He

Library and Archives Canada Cataloguing in Publication

He, Bing, date
Alphabet zen / Bing He.

Poems.
ISBN 1-894770-23-4

I. Title.

PS8615.E12A64 2005   C811'.6   C2005-901570-5

Printed in Canada by Coach House Printing

TSAR Publications
P.O. Box 6996, Station A
Toronto, Onatrio M5W 1X7
Canada

www.tsarbooks.com

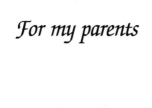

For my parents

Acknowledgement

Earlier versions of "Cyclist and Crow" and "Target Pistol" appeared in *Writual,* "Untitled Apples" appeared in *Xcp, Cross Culture Poetics,* "Colours" in the anthology *So Let you Know.*

I would like to thank Betty Warrington-Kearsley, Michael Kearsley, Stephanie Bolster and Seymour Mayne for their feedback and encouragement at different stages of this book.

I would also like to thank the City of Ottawa for the art grant of poetry writing in 2002.

Contents

Alphabet Zen

<pre>
                    A
               R R
             O   C
           O   H
         F   I
       O   T
     F   E
   T   b r i d g e s   C
     E   T
       M   H
         P   E
           L   A
         E   D
</pre>

B(eing)

Behind the door
Before a road
Beneath the sand
Beside a well
Between bubbles
Beyond death

C

The cold fresh melon
munched by children
Only a slice of its skins
left in the sky glistens

D

a
kid
in
red
tries
to
build
God
with
sand
while
wind
is
mad

E

A yellow bee
spins the red lanterns on an apple tree
above the green weeds

f

through the sound holes
of a violin
unfolds

G

the arrow sign
journeyed around the earth
to its origin

H

Two solitary telephone poles

c

a

n

be connected through the wire?

I

Even a section of bamboo stem
has a capital I

J

How tiring the fishhook
Always sharp and tense
Why not relax

K

Kafka's
Key to
K
Clicked
Quick for a peek!

L

Man
erect
gazes
at his
own shadow. Two beings
are fastened into one painting

M

Moon		Moving
Motionless		Moving
	Mountain	
Moving	Moving	Moving

N

Nothing
Not even the eyes of a dragonfly
Notice the inner
Noise of
Nothingness

O

sun earth moon rotates each other into a big void

To draw wind
a flag scribbles some abstract lines

Q

The seagull breaks the waves of ocean
when the sun rises

r

the little bud
stretches its arms
to embrace
the first breeze of spring

S

So

Sleek

So

Subtle

Sails

Swan's

Slender

Shadow

Slowly

Swaying

The reed is long gone
Its reflection still remembered
in the water

U (you)

Sphinx'
perpetual gaze
hollows
your pupil
into a statue

V

– When winter comes, wild geese fly to south

V   V

   V   V

   V   V

     V   V

       V   V

        V V

          V

W

Mountain
Turns itself upside-down when it sees its reflection on
Water

X

The cross road-sign
at the crossroad
is blown by the wind to an

at the entrance of the road

Y

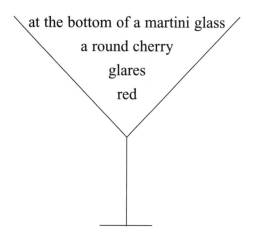

at the bottom of a martini glass
a round cherry
glares
red

Z

Cicadas
waken
the dozing summer noon
with sizzling

ZZZZZZZZZZZZZZZZZZZZZZ

Sketches

I

Water
    disfigures
the iris
      in a glass
                A blue
        melody
     streaming
out

II

A streetlight turns on its tap
the streams of light
are washing off
a triangle of
night

III

a white page
o p e n s
the w or l d
d i s appears
i n s i d e
l e a v i n g
black traces

IV

By turning time
u p s i d e
down

sand
r e f i l l s
the old vacancy

V

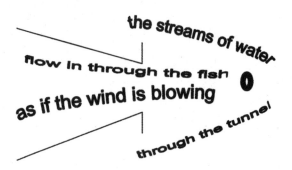

VI

```
l
    e    a
    v
e    s                              birds
shu    tter              sing
      on          on
    branches
    The dead
    old trunk
    awakened
    by noises
```

VII   A spread body's dream

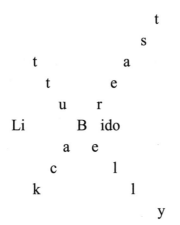

```
                              t
                        s
        t               a
          t         e
            u     r
  Li          B   ido
          a     e
        c         l
      k                 l
                          y
```

Snow

branches
brushing
moon
glistening
flakes
fall   i   n
   i   g   n   g
i   n   g

        g

I step into the glowing land
surrounded by the drifting stars

Reflections

$$\frac{\text{WIND}}{\text{MI}\text{И}\text{D}}$$

Immigration – Transformation – Assimilation

Word Sonnets

(1)

He
grips
her
hip
She
nibbles
his
lips
until
the
baby
clips
the
ad

(2) A Crying Girl

She
swallowed
an
orange
seed

Her
stomach
aches
for
fear
of
an
orange
tree

(3)

The
moon
rises
for
children
to
fly
a
white
balloon
in
their
black
dreams

(4)

He
finds
solace
in
silence
broken
by
the
whistle
of
ambulance
echoing
his
scream

(5) First time

maple
leaves
bleed
in
the
window

a
girl
paints
red
in
a
messy
bed

Cyclist and Crow

– After Alex Colville's Painting Cyclist and Crow

Is
Bird
Flying
Or
Bike
Rolling

Or
Both
Bike & Bird
Gliding

World
Pauses
When
Cyclist
And bird
Look at
Each
Other

There is no
Bird, nor
Bike

Only the waving ocean of reed flowers
You just blinked

Target Pistol and Man

– After Alex Colville's Painting *Target Pistol and Man*

A black hole
with silver rim
from a black steel pistol
pointing at you

Two black pupils
with white cornea
from the black-clothed man
staring at you

The two folded hands under the chin
will they open up and press the trigger
to make a real hole on the canvas
or it will be pointed at his own head
blossoms like the bullet through an apple

Train and Horse

– After Alex Colville's Painting *Train and Horse*

Lust
metamorphoses
into
a black horse
lurking
on the train tracks –
the silver scars
are stitched
extend to the end
where
a piercing light
rumbles
    Lone
      Lone

approaching

Night Walk

– After Alex Corville's Painting Night Walk

Darkness
awakened by the vibration

of sound
coming from

two black leather shoes
trampling on stone paved lanes

in rhythm of
a dog's heavy breath

disquiets
the blind eyes

His walking stick pokes
the abyss

Leaves suddenly turn pale
withered

The End

– After Alex Colville's Painting *Swimmer*

The sky is already dead

Where the wounded sun still bleeds

Ocean is reflecting upon the consequences of the fading lights

While a gigantic head wrapped with bandage slowly emerges

Its hollow gaze transfixes the last tides into waving sand

Untitled Apples

I

Falling
from the white jade plate[1]
through the black hole
A red apple
splashes the earth into
an autumn harvest

Moon breaks
Earth reborn

II

An apple tree
dancing upon my tomb
knocks at the coffin
with its round ripe thumps
pump, pump...

I wake up from the reality
entering a red-scented dream

[1] As a child, I didn't know it was the moon and called it white jade plate.

– Li Po

III

Dropped from a branch,
An absent minded apple
pounds on wisdom's white head.
Startled,
    it flies away
            higher &
            higher
radiates in the sky of human minds.

What beautiful sunshine!

IV

*A*dam
*P*uts his heart on a plate, slices it into
*P*ieces for you to taste his sour
*L*onging for
*E*den

V

"You have an apple
I have an apple
If we exchange
You and I have one each.

You have an idea
I have an idea
If we tell each other
We both have two."

"Which do you choose?" the teacher asks.
"Idea!" the pupils exclaim.

But if you have an apple
and an idea
I will choose the apple
instead

VI

"Love apple," Mom says,
"it is good for you."
I gaze at her skin red
till it flushes into a tomato.

Colours

Red

A frozen strawberry in my mouth
shrieks the flame –
"Cool!"

Black

Sinking in eternity
the old well closes its lid
motionlessly

Yellow

Ironing my heart
Sunbeams smooth the wrinkles
of old sorrow

Purple

Nocturne resonates the dream
of violets
in an April night

Green

To keep winter fresh
mint cools the snow
under the grass

White

Moon washed
in a pond of
black ink

Blue

Your reflecting eyes –
ocean and sky,
one

Life

Ashes
fly
on the flaming field wild
Out of clear blue smoke

here comes a black
butterfly

Chocolate Croissant

The creamy body
slices open

A white steam
screams

You chocolate her
puffy tummy

Closing Time

The last train lashes the tunnel
leaves fumes and ashes flying

Stepping on the platform
He carries his belongings
walks towards the gate
where the iron door is falling

The vertical and horizontal bars stop him
dismember his silhouette against lightning

Snow Keeps Falling

Houses suddenly age overnight
Chimneys cough with short breathes

Snow keeps falling

Vehicle fumes intoxicate the air
People sleepwalk by, not knowing why

Snow keeps falling

The bell strikes noon in monotone
The grey sky pours lead relentlessly

Snow keeps falling

White dots erase the pedestrians one by one
Wind ploughs roads into open ditches

Snow keeps falling

The darkened earth slips into coma
Breath is frozen into mist hanging

Snow keeps falling

falling, falling on the immense cemetery
A black crow lands on blinding whiteness

stunned by eternity

Snow keeps falling

The Last Sight

An invalid
nods
under the arch

electrified
by a piercing hoot
Trembling,

he opens his eyes
The pouring black ink from the sky
submerges the buildings, the streets, the trees

He gasps for breath
while two white dots
of an owl's eyes
coldly
stare

Branches and Moon

leafy branches dusting
    the moon
    to mirror
landscape of my iris -
    a black sun drowned
    in twinkling grey ripples
I squint

    A stream of tears overflows into
    rain

    Moon cleansed

Street Night

The red eyes of cars wink under the dark
alluring solitary shadows to the corner

Red brick walls are bruised by neon lights
then licked by the wet tongues of rain

Telephone poles dig deep into the dike
one night's discharge overflows the pavements

A chimney erupts in the last scream of orgasm
flaming wood shudders into black ashes

Night

Stone stairs
blue
under the moon
Wind
swirls
collecting echoes
of memory
Black leaves
sneak
in a soundless alley

An old crow on the branch suddenly awakes
"Ga –"
It shatters the streetlight's orange dream

Above the foot long weeds

the iron knob
rusty & still
locks the season
outside

Shadows of cracked wooden fences
abandoned by the parting sun
creep into the cabin
through the crack
under the door

and quickly withdraw

Midnight

Darkness descends under the wings of crows

Bald trees spread their troops in rows
Raising the spears above their heads

The sullen river arches it back
Climbing silently on the bank

Now! A cat commands

The church raises its spire
Strikes fiercely
1! 2! 3!
        ...12!

To shed faint lights
through the broken holes
in the sky

One Afternoon

– After Pierre Boogaerts' Photo Series *Une après-midi sur mon balcon, Montréal, 18 août 1978*

a closed door
    an empty chair

  shadows of black leaves
on the page of an open book

      the parched wall
a calling

        from beyond
          the horizon

a glimpse of a curtained window
          a moment

I cannot re-enter

Un Chanson d'Amour

Lying on your lap, I count
stripping leaves
one by one
fling as memory drifts away
Petals
swirling down on the ground
the crackling sound
strikes
the bell in your chest
vibrating mine
                    – "Don't go!"
Wind chases the echo
of your footsteps in a black lane

Sunset carves your image on the white wall
You come back everyday when the sun says good-bye

One Night Alone

Turning on the lamp
The light spreads its orange skirt

Arabian music is vibrating its belly
up, down   back, front

A glass of wine releases crimson
from the pressed lips

Don't stir
let the curtain fall

Another star
sinks into the bed of

Loneliness

Wind Flower Snow Moon[2]

– A Love Story of a Chinese Girl in Ancient Time

Wind

Allured by the aroma of lilac
She pushed the window open to touch
the first pink of spring

A young man roaming
raised his head

A glance –

cracked the brick wall
Her black hair splashed
in the stream of wind

---

[2] *Wind Flower Snow Moon* is a Chinese idiom meaning sexual love. In ancient China, marriage was arranged by parents. Love affairs were prohibited. This poem uses four themes of traditional Chinese play: meeting, longing, separation and reunion, to describe a girl's courageous deed in a love story.

Flower

Lotus
stretching
her petals
at dusk
pa, pa
Dew
wet
ovary

I will blossom
under his touch

Snow

Passing through
the narrow alley
the grey brick walls
the brown leaf-covered yard
the red-carved wooden window frames

to her

Then no message

Winter fell

with his thousand words in floating snowflakes

Moon

Tonight
the moon is full
so are my breasts
round with desire
Come
Don't let the beautiful night
slip by

Dusk of Yuan Ming Garden[3]

Brown lotus leaves are burning
humming their swan song
in a black soiled pond

A narrow dusty trail
winds under withered leaves
disappears among bald trees

A light blue smoke rises
from the cane chimney
into the flaming sky

Broken marble columns standing
in their shadows, witness
the rise and fall of this land

The sun is branded
by the autumn scene
at dusk of Yuan Ming Garden

[3] Yuan Ming Garden, the imperial summer palace, also called "the garden of gardens", was built by six generations of Ching emperors. The Garden, spanned a three-hundred-fifty hectare area with treasure collected over two thousand years in China, was looted and then torched by British and French armies (ordered by Lord Elgin) in 1860 in Beijing, where ruins still exist.

A Business Call from a Chinese Woman

I could tell through the phone
that you are Chinese from your accent
You asked for some data
then told me in Mandarin
that you are from Taiwan
  a beautiful island evergreen
and living in Whitehorse
  ice doesn't melt there in June

I do not know the extreme
that veins can carry
from frying heat
to freezing cold
But you made it
happily found a place
where it is safe

You migrated
from one place to another
      mainland China
        Taiwan
          United States
            Canada
  like a little sparrow
    flying
      further
      further
        away
from your homeland
The bird can fly to south to warm up
when winter returns
You will remain
forever
amid deep snow and the howling wind

Sitting by the fireplace
let the memory flap the wing
You told your children stories
of that ancient world
      Moon-Cakes in fall
      Dragon boats in May
Or the Cow Man Star and the Weaving Lady Star
can only meet on the Milky Way
on the seventh month, seventh day[4]

One day
you will become a story —
a stone grey
shivering in immense whiteness
Your great-grand children
puzzled
asking in English
why you walked
that far
to
your fate

[4] Chinese legend: a fairy girl who was good at weaving in the sky fell in love with a
cow man on earth. She landed on earth and married him and they had two children.
But the Mother of Heaven Temple was infuriated by her absence and called her
back. She had no choice but to obey. While the Weaving Lady was flying with the
Mother, the Cow Man, carrying their children, followed them to the sky. The
Mother found out and took out her hairpin and drew a line. Suddenly the line
became a river with mighty waves, the Silver River (Milky Way). The Cow Man and
Weaving Lady were separated in the sky. Only on the seventh day of the seventh
month, all magpies in the universe fly to the Silver River to form a bridge so that
Cow Man and Weaving Lady can cross the river and meet each other once a year.

When Chinese Writing Poetry in English

I cannot shake up these letters
so that they can shape into pictures

I cannot put one man on top of two so that people unite
I cannot plant a tree among others where a forest grows

You can see the bird in Chinese flapping its feathers
The horse gallops with four hoofs in the air
Water drips from the roof in a rainy day
A sad heart roams alone in the autumn

A flat line stretches the horizon thin and wide
A vertical dash exclaims an upright tree
A slanting stroke floats like a swaying wave
Seeping through from upper left, streaming out of lower right

I cannot narrate the steps of thousands of years' journey -
The first carvings on the turtle bones predict danger or luck
Writing on bamboo strips forms the test vertical
Black ink on embroidered silk traces the dragon's dance
The printing and papermaking enlightened the west

I cannot transform the moon into a background
Sung with clapping hands to a billion poems
Danced to by Li Po's drunk steps after litres of wine
I cannot outline its concave and convex
The emotion tides on sleeplessly nights
Till the withered wives finally rejoin their men

I cannot take you up to the mountain on Double Ninth Day
Drink wine with autumn wind then splash ink on rice paper
        into a painting
Nor can I lead you through the meadows on Ching Ming Day

Burn paper money for the dead while enjoying the new green
     of spring

Each dish, each street name, each proverb
Is a poem entangled with stories of ancient dynasties
Each coin, each painting, each temple
Depicts the harmony of earth, sky and the human beings

English letters twist, like tadpoles wriggling their tails
Producing endless bubbles, burst one by one in the stream
Before I grasp their meanings, everything is gone into the
     water

The Carpet Room

– To a Carpet Shop Owner in Istanbul

You sit
in the centre of the room
with the carpets piled up to the roof
You talk
to each carpet
Hereke, Persian, Oucha
as if you were
talking to your students
about Yeats, Shelley and T.S.Eliot

In the room the women come and go
Talking of Michelangelo

In your room
people come to discuss
knots per square inch, is it
a natural dye, made of cotton or wool
You know each piece
as if the features of your girls
the ruby red, the sky blue
like Esra's lips and Selda's eyes

In the room the women come and go
Talking of Michelangelo

Eighteen years
the world swirling around you
You remain
in the carpet room
like an ageless sculpture

The echo of youthful voices
reciting poetry
grows louder and louder
until it shatters you
In your grey-haired dreams
you start to mumble

In the room the women come and go
Talking of Michelangelo

The Ideal Woman

– After Amedeo Modigliani's *Nude*

The curve of her slender waist
Draws the outline of a tempting land
Where a round tummy glows desire

Her private hair tucked between two thighs
Grows pub(l)ic(ly) under lustful stares
Tangle with pythons and serpents

Her arms spread open with yes
Her head tilts to half-yielding no
Her c-cup breasts protrude for caress
Yet pressed lips form a *who-knows*

She baths in the sunbeams purified by the legends
Her luring singing leads sailors under reefs at night
Baudelaire consumed her perfume like an alcoholic
Gentlemen in suits dined with her naked on grass
Byron couldn't utter a word if she didn't whisper
Picasso was just a bullfighter without her touch

I wish that she could wake up
Not by the kiss of a handsome prince
Nor by the seduction of a luscious apple
Just open her eyes and look around
How does she feel? Is she satisfied?
Why year after year she is up there
Painted as a fleshy *nature morte*
Forever young body, forever old theme

A muscular girl with short spiky hair
Snatches the brush and kicks the painter
Screams a fist-clenched "fuck!"

This is the City

This is the city
where the sky is blue and the air is fresh
where grass is green and flowers are red
where roads are straight and streetlights are bright
where you can never see a fight

This is the city where every pedestrian stops at the red light
This is the city where all politicians are politically correct
This is the city where beggars wish you a nice day
But the passengers in elevators are quiet
This is the city

This is the city where lonely dwellers swamp in bars, gulp beer
        after beer,
where girls puff cigarettes, no one dares say hi, just look at
        each other with white vacant stares.
This is the city where bar-goers go back to their apartments
        with clothes stinking of cigarette,
neck on neck with a stranger or have a safe, clean, trouble-
        free masturbation.
This is the city where lips murmur, arms stretch, legs spread,
        breasts protrude,
from TV, from magazines, from ads, from books, from movies,
        screaming: take me!
But hey, No means No, otherwise you are in trouble.

This is the city where one hand flips the TV's remote control
        and the other clicks on a computer's mouse
This is the city where telecommunication is booming and
        person-to-person contact is sliding

This is the city where every newspaper has the same face and
    all reporters read in monotone
This is the city where junk food is eaten, junk shows watched
    and junk mail circulated

This is the city that is ranked the best place in the world
It has the safest streets on earth
It has the most polite people you can meet
It also has first-class boredom in the universe